THE

HILLARY BIBLE

a Conspiracy Theory

Donald Trump

could be proud of

S.R. Smith, Hs.D

Critical Acclaim for The Hillary Bible:

"Hillary Clinton is obviously willing to use any trick in the book, including the Good Book, to advance her devious plot to improve the lives of the undeserving."
Amy Johansson – Forest Lake, MN

"With this latest conspiracy theory, Donald Trump proves once again that he's a master at creating cleverly crafted scenarios to undermine his enemies."
Josh Waterson – Redondo Beach, CA

"Donald Trump's accusations may sound far-fetched, like that whole Birther thing, but I've never read the Bible, so maybe Hillary actually did make all this 'love your neighbor' stuff up . It sure sounds like Hillary's agenda to me."
Ned Stephens – Omaha, NE

"What's truly frightening about all this is how the falsified passages inserted by the Clinton Campaign sound so convincingly Biblical. One could almost convince oneself that one had heard these pronouncements somewhere before."
Dr. Jonas Peabody – Essex, England

More Critical Acclaim for The Hillary Bible:

"It's hard to believe that even Hillary would stoop so low as to attribute ridiculous nonsense like 'I was a stranger and you welcomed me' to our Lord and Savior. Donald Trump has exposed her lies and will keep us safe by keeping those Godless strangers out of our country."

Joan Franks – Albany, NY

"This is a very important book. For the sake of our families and the American way of life, we need to root out this evil in all of its sinister iterations. Under my leadership, the Deacons at our church are putting together a well regulated militia to seek and destroy every single copy of these blasphemy-filled abominations disguised as our Sacred Texts."

Rev. Bo Thurman – Tyler, TX

Dedicated to ghostwriters, those unsung heroes of the non-fiction genre, who occasionally regret their complicity in creating false narratives for their clients

CONTENTS

Foreword

When Donald Trump says that he's a Christian, I'm pretty sure what he means is that he's not a Muslim. Or a Jew. I'd be very surprised if he's actually given any thought to what it means to be a Christian. I'd be even more surprised if he has ever actually read an entire passage of the Holy Bible. As I understand it, he is far too busy making deals and bragging about his questionable accomplishments to read anything much longer than a tweet.

So it occurred to me that if one of his advisors, one of his best people told him that Jesus never actually taught love, tolerance and humility, he would have no reason to doubt that assertion. The next logical step in his suspicious, manipulative mind might be to develop a conspiracy theory aimed directly at his current enemy: Hillary Clinton.

The theory goes like this:

> Hillary makes up some fake biblical passages which support her own crooked agenda (love your neighbor, turn the other cheek, do unto others, etc.).

> Hillary conspires with Liberal publishers to print counterfeit Bibles which include these fabricated quotations attributed to our Lord and Savior.

Hillary conspires with Liberal clergy across America to promote these lies to their flock in an effort to discredit the Donald's claim to Christianity and undermine his bid for the highest office in the land.

Then the Donald, as he does when he realizes that what he wants to say won't fit into a tweet, hires a ghost writer to elaborate on his conspiracy theory and bolster his claim that he is a good Christian deserving of the votes of his fellow believers.

While this fictional exploration of the Donald's latest conspiracy theory may seem far-fetched, it is no more preposterous than his insinuations that President Obama is a Muslim non-citizen who uses his high office to collaborate with terrorists. It is no more delusional than his claim that he will force Mexico to pay for a wall that he can personally will into existence, or that he, alone, will bring an end (yes, he said "end") to crime and violence, and that he will single-handedly make America safe on his very first day in office. But of all of his outrageous claims that are completely unrelated to the true, the real, or the possible, his assertion that he is a Christian – a follower and devotee of the man who taught us to love our neighbors as ourselves – is arguably the most egregious lie he has ever told.

An earlier incarnation of this book, titled "13 Blasphemies", was a more general satirical treatise on the difference between certain political positions and the words of Jesus. Now that there is a very real threat that the Donald might be our next president, I resurrected the general concept and format to shed light on his hypocrisy for undecided Christian readers.

Donald Trump is a very dangerous man who is feeding on the fear and hatred of his misguided and gullible followers. This book is an attempt to illustrate the vast chasm between the Donald's hateful rhetoric and the Christian ethics which form the foundation of so many Americans' lives. Please, for the love of Jesus, do not allow this petty, vengeful, self-serving, hollow shell of a man become the President of the United States.

S. R. Smith, Hs.D

Acknowledgement

My heartfelt thanks in advance to Donald Trump for not suing me. In the unthinkable event that he actually becomes president, my sincere thanks, again in advance, for not imprisoning me for treason. Please note that I have been very clear that this book is not written by (duh!), sanctioned by, or approved by Donald J. Trump.

Introduction

First of all, let me tell you – I am a Christian. Anyone who knows me can tell you I'm a Christian: my beautiful children, my beautiful wife, lots of people, lots of important people will tell you – I'm a Christian.

Now, I've been telling you all along there's something going on, and I have proof. Believe me, I have proof. And you wouldn't believe some of the people who are involved in this thing. Hillary Clinton, of course, but several other very high-level people whose names you would recognize. Believe me, you know who they are – it's unbelievable! And the conspiracy these people have committed would blow your mind. You won't believe what these people – and these are devious people – you won't believe what these people have done.

They have actually added – and this is amazing – they have taken the Holy Bible and added false quotes, actually inserted totally fabricated text into the Good Book and attributed these ridiculous statements to Jesus Christ. It's outrageous, I know, but believe me they have done this. The Hillary Clinton campaign has worked with well-known publishers – and you wouldn't believe who's involved in this – to print counterfeit copies of the Holy Bible containing statements which we know, we absolutely know Jesus could never have uttered.

Then, the Clinton people distributed these very Bibles to known Liberals, well-known Liberal Clerics whose congregations are riddled with Democrats and issued instructions, very specific instructions to these Liberal clerics to read these totally, totally fabricated passages to their parishioners to turn their people against me.

Now, when you read these lies – and I'll break them down for you in this amazing, amazing book – when you read these total lies it will be crystal clear to you that the point of this whole conspiracy is of course, obviously to slander my sterling reputation as a rich and powerful Christian.

I've got very smart, and I mean very, very smart people working on this thing day and night, and they have assured me that is it absolutely, positively true that the Bibles they looked into are counterfeit, and they have rock-solid evidence that these forgeries can be directly traced back to Hillary Clinton, who is a known criminal. You don't need to take my word for it, the FBI called her a criminal and the delegates to the Republican National Convention, who we know are excellent, excellent judges of character, pronounced her Guilty.

My experts, who are top experts in the field of Biblical history, absolutely the best, have told me that the false quotes inserted by Clinton's people are not even remotely, remotely believable in the context of what we know Jesus said. It's just a bunch of lies they made up. And I'll give them credit; the language they used really almost sounds like the genuine article, almost, but the stuff they made up is obviously aimed at me, personally, and designed to make people question my sincere devotion to Jesus Christ and all that he stands for. And none of it is true, believe me, it's just not true.

One of the cleverest things the Clinton people did, and again I give them credit for how clever they were with this thing, is that they made up three different versions of their lies to make them sound like they fit with the style of different versions of the Bible that they distributed to various Liberal Clerics based on the version they usually use. To help you understand how truly, truly dishonest these people are, I included all three different versions of the false, absolutely false passages to show you just how disgustingly manipulative these people are.

Let me give you an example of what I did throughout this remarkable book:

The King James Version – Luke 6:29

And unto him that smiteth thee on the [one] cheek offer also the other; and him that taketh away thy cloke forbid not [to take thy] coat also.

The New Revised Standard Version– Luke 6:29

If anyone strikes you on the cheek, offer the other also; and from anyone who takes away your coat do not withhold even your shirt.

The New Living Translation – Luke 6:29

If someone slaps you on one cheek, offer the other cheek also. If someone demands your coat, offer your shirt also.

You see how I've given you the opportunity to see exactly how deceptive and cunning the Clinton people have been, creating these different versions of the same lie, the very same lie with a slightly different pseudo-biblical style to appeal to the full spectrum of hard-working, honest Americans, regardless of the translation of the Good Book they are used to hearing.

This is also a great example of exactly, precisely the kind of twisting of the truth that Clinton's people are trying to accomplish. Notice how the message here is that – and this is obviously ridiculous – the message is that Jesus doesn't want us to keep and bear arms to protect ourselves and our property. This is clearly, obviously a personal attack on me and my position on gun laws and it is outrageous, absolutely outrageous that Hillary would stoop so low as to infuse false doctrine into this campaign in order to feed her own voracious appetite for power and recognition.

Now, let me be crystal clear: America is a Christian nation founded on Christian principles and one of our most sacred Christian principles is codified in the Second Amendment. If Jesus didn't want us to fight for our rights and our property with handguns and semi-automatic weapons – which of course he would have wanted – then how could we possibly call ourselves a Christian nation? Obviously we could not.

This book is full of examples, many examples of obvious contradictions like the one I just gave you, which demonstrate how totally ridiculous and unbelievable the lies inserted in the bogus Bibles by the Clinton campaign really, truly are.

It will probably come as no surprise to you that I actually did not write this book, since I didn't write any of the books I have taken credit for over the years. I didn't even write this introduction, but since I don't read books, my ghost writer figured I would never know about this confession, especially if he put it into the second-last paragraph of the introduction. Introductions are for losers, anyway.

This is a truly, truly great book that exposes Hillary Clinton for the weak and crooked politician she really is and makes it absolutely, positively, crystal clear to anyone who reads it that absolutely nothing, and I mean nothing Jesus Christ ever said or did would call into question my integrity and credibility as a shrewd, rich, powerful, take-no-prisoners, winner-take-all Christian.

Donald J Trump (as imagined by S.R. Smith and not reviewed or approved by Mr. Trump or anyone else)

Hillary's First Lie

Turn the Other Cheek

The King James Version

Luke 6

[27] But I say unto you which hear, Love your enemies, do good to them which hate you,

[28] Bless them that curse you, and pray for them which despitefully use you.

[29] And unto him that smiteth thee on the [one] cheek offer also the other; and him that taketh away thy cloke forbid not [to take thy] coat also.

[30] Give to every man that asketh of thee; and of him that taketh away thy goods ask [them] not again.

The New Revised Standard Version

Luke 6

[27] 'But I say to you that listen, Love your enemies, do good to those who hate you,

[28]bless those who curse you, pray for those who abuse you.

[29]If anyone strikes you on the cheek, offer the other also; and from anyone who takes away your coat do not withhold even your shirt.

[30]Give to everyone who begs from you; and if anyone takes away your goods, do not ask for them again.

The New Living Translation

Luke 6

27"But to you who are willing to listen, I say, love your enemies! Do good to those who hate you.

28 Bless those who curse you. Pray for those who hurt you.

29 If someone slaps you on one cheek, offer the other cheek also. If someone demands your coat, offer your shirt also.

30 Give to anyone who asks; and when things are taken away from you, don't try to get them back.

Hillary's Crooked Agenda

She thinks she can trick voters into believing that my strong position the Second Amendment is not supported by Holy Scripture

She wants to leave honest, hard-working Americans vulnerable to attacks by illegal immigrant rapists and Muslim refugees as part of her conspiracy with Obama

Donald Trump's Truth

This is so obviously a direct, personal attack on me and my support of Second Amendment rights that any Bible scholar would recognize it, and recognize it immediately, as an absolute fabrication. Hillary wants you to believe that Jesus said if some Mexican walks into your house, slaps you around and takes your stuff, you should do nothing to defend yourself and your property! In fact, she goes so far as to tell us that Jesus, that's Jesus Christ, not "Hey-Zeus", wants us to go get more of our stuff and give it to this low-life immigrant! This one seems pretty important to the Clinton campaign, because they threw it into Matthew, too, in a slightly altered but very recognizable variation, very recognizable.

This is just more solid proof that Hillary wants to dismantle the Second Amendment and alter its meaning to emphasize that inconsequential, and I mean totally meaningless phrase at the beginning - something about a well regulated militia.

Supreme Court Justice Antonin Scalia – who was by the way a good friend of mine and a well-known Biblical scholar, a very good friend – he knew that since America is a Christian nation, founded on Christian principles, he knew that Jesus would have been a strong supporter, very strong supporter of using guns for self-defense. Which is why Scalia said in his decision in DC v Heller, that our right to keep and bear arms is totally unrelated to a well regulated militia, totally unrelated. This man knew the Bible and the Constitution inside and out and he told us – and when a man like Scalia talks we need to listen – he told us that the Constitution gives us the right to use guns to protect ourselves and our property. Which is why only a total loser would believe that Jesus ever said "turn the other cheek".

So don't believe this nonsense even for a second, because it's a slippery slope that ends up with the Clinton government taking away our fundamental right to shoot the immigrant scum who would violate our God-given right to get very rich – which, by the way, I am: very, very rich – and preserve the place of native-born Americans as the rightful owners of these United States.

By the way, it gets even more ridiculous. At the beginning of this particular fake passage, Hillary's fake passage writers made the totally unbelievable claim that we should LOVE our enemies! I'm not kidding; she thinks American voters are stupid enough to believe that our Lord and Savior actually said we should love our enemies. Unbelievable! I'll give you more detail in the Second Lie chapter, because the Clinton campaign also snuck in the crazy notion of loving your enemies in Matthew 5.

Hillary's Second Lie

Love Your Enemies

The King James Version

Matthew 5

⁴³ Ye have heard that it hath been said, Thou shalt love thy neighbour, and hate thine enemy.

⁴⁴ But I say unto you, Love your enemies, bless them that curse you, do good to them that hate you, and pray for them which despitefully use you, and persecute you;

⁴⁵ That ye may be the children of your Father which is in heaven: for he maketh his sun to rise on the evil and on the good, and sendeth rain on the just and on the unjust.

⁴⁶ For if ye love them which love you, what reward have ye? do not even the publicans the same?

⁴⁷ And if ye salute your brethren only, what do ye more [than others]? do not even the publicans so?

The New Revised Standard Version

Matthew 5

43 'You have heard that it was said, "You shall love your neighbour and hate your enemy."

44But I say to you, Love your enemies and pray for those who persecute you,

45so that you may be children of your Father in heaven; for he makes his sun rise on the evil and on the good, and sends rain on the righteous and on the unrighteous.

46For if you love those who love you, what reward do you have? Do not even the tax-collectors do the same?

47And if you greet only your brothers and sisters, what more are you doing than others? Do not even the Gentiles do the same?

The New Living Translation

Matthew 5

[43] "You have heard the law that says, 'Love your neighbor' and hate your enemy.

[44] But I say, love your enemies! Pray for those who persecute you!

[45] In that way, you will be acting as true children of your Father in heaven. For he gives his sunlight to both the evil and the good, and he sends rain on the just and the unjust alike.

[46] If you love only those who love you, what reward is there for that? Even corrupt tax collectors do that much.

[47] If you are kind only to your friends, how are you different from anyone else? Even pagans do that.

Hillary's Crooked Agenda

She's trying to make America question my brilliant plan – and it is completely brilliant – to keep Muslims out of America

She wants to allow Mexican immigrant rapists and murderers to roam free, all across America spreading their crime spree across all 50 states

She wants to export American jobs to low-wage workers in third world countries – places so disgusting no self-respecting person would ever want to live there

Donald Trump's Truth

This lie is so over-the-top, I can't believe even Hillary has the – well she doesn't have those (or does she?) – but I can't believe she has the guts to say that Jesus Christ told us to love our enemies. It's just ridiculous. But you know why she said it, right? Because I hate my enemies – hate them – and I hate America's enemies. And what she's doing is trying to drive a wedge between me and America's Christian majority.

Now let me be perfectly clear: America has enemies, lots of enemies. And make no mistake; the three most dangerous enemies are:

Muslims – not all Muslims, just most of them

Mexican immigrants, who are mostly criminals

Foreign low-wage workers who have stolen jobs from patriotic Americans.

Let me break it down for you. First, the Muslims. Muslims are not Christians, definitely not Christians. And America is a Christian nation, founded on Christian principles. That fact alone should make it clear that these people are our sworn enemies. Now, as everyone knows – everyone but the godless Muslims – everyone knows that Jesus Christ was the founder of the Christian Church. So let's get real: a guy who was smart enough to build something as amazing as Christianity would not have been dumb enough to say "love your enemies". That's just ridiculous – completely ridiculous.

Now, it goes without saying that Mexican immigrants are our enemies. As we all know, most of them are criminals of some kind, usually rapists and murderers. And the few that aren't criminals most definitely know who the criminals are and where they are hiding. Believe me, a friend of my enemy is my enemy, believe me.

So don't believe for a minute that Jesus – and again I mean Jesus Christ, not some guy named "Hey-Zeus" – don't believe for a minute that Jesus wants us to love these people. They are cutting a swath of crime, terrible crime across America and the only solution is to round them up and send them back where they came from, and believe me that's not America.

Foreign low-wage workers, they're not a direct threat to our safety, but make no mistake – they are our enemies who, by the way, I do not love. These people, these little foreign people are willing to work for a tiny fraction of what American workers need. Not because they need to feed their families. No, these unseen enemies take your jobs – take food from the tables of honest, decent people here in the United States – because they hate America.

The Clinton campaign concocted this lie about loving your foreign worker enemies – which they attribute to our Lord and Savior, which is clearly ridiculous – to discredit me and my pledge, which I will keep, believe me, I will bring high-paying manufacturing jobs back to the people who deserve them – you – by taking them from our enemies who hate us.

Hillary's Third Lie

He who lives by the sword shall die by the sword

The King James Version

Matthew 26

[52] Then said Jesus unto him, Put up again thy sword into his place: for all they that take the sword shall perish with the sword.

[53] Thinkest thou that I cannot now pray to my Father, and he shall presently give me more than twelve legions of angels?

[54] But how then shall the scriptures be fulfilled, that thus it must be?

The New Revised Standard Version

Matthew 26

⁵²Then Jesus said to him, 'Put your sword back into its place; for all who take the sword will perish by the sword.

⁵³Do you think that I cannot appeal to my Father, and he will at once send me more than twelve legions of angels?

⁵⁴But how then would the scriptures be fulfilled, which say it must happen in this way?'

The New Living Translation

Matthew 26

[52] "Put away your sword," Jesus told him. "Those who use the sword will die by the sword.

[53] Don't you realize that I could ask my Father for thousands of angels to protect us, and he would send them instantly?

[54] But if I did, how would the Scriptures be fulfilled that describe what must happen now?"

Hillary's Crooked Agenda

She's trying to get the American electorate to believe the ridiculous, totally ridiculous lie that Jesus was non-violent

She wants to take guns away from American Christians so they can't defend themselves against the Obama-led Muslim jihadist conspiracy

Donald Trump's Truth

This is another totally ridiculous lie inserted into the Good Book by the Clinton campaign. The implication that Jesus was a non-violent man – which he was not, by the way – is obviously another attack on me personally and my crusade to prevent Hillary and her stupid Liberal minions from abolishing the Second Amendment to our sacred Constitution.

If you look at this in combination with that ridiculous nonsense – and it is totally ridiculous – about turning the other cheek, you can see where they're going with this thing. Hillary wants you to surrender your weapons to her administration to complete her quest – and believe me, she's on a quest – to complete her quest to take away your freedom and consolidate her own power for her own crooked purposes. After she takes all of your guns, she plans to ruin your life by raising the minimum wage, guaranteeing health care to you and your children and making sure that your kids can go to college.

You see folks, when patriotic Americans have guns, they can protect themselves – protect themselves from illegal immigrants and Muslims, sure – but the main thing real American patriots need to protect themselves from is the American government. Because real patriots know that their government is a basically evil institution whose main purpose is to deprive them of their God-given, Christian rights. And make no mistake; the most fundamental right of every Christian is to keep and bear arms.

And when patriotic American Christians are armed to the teeth, only then can the protect themselves from the government – a government that, I'm telling you has come completely off the rails – only then can they protect themselves from this out-of-control government that wants them to earn a living wage, and have quality, affordable health care and education.

Don't let this crooked woman pervert your Christian heritage with lies – and believe me they are lies – about our Lord and Savior being some kind of non-violent Gandhi-man. Our Christian Founding Fathers knew very well that Jesus intended for us to keep and bear arms and made that sacred right the centerpiece of the US Constitution.

You've heard Hillary talking about how Canada's level of gun ownership is only 10 percent of our own. Then she tells us that the murder rate in Canada – also 10 percent of ours by the way – has something to do with gun ownership, completely ignoring the totally obvious fact that the pathetically under-armed Canadians were totally unprepared for the Canadian government's take-over of their health care system. Obviously, if more Canadians owned guns, Canada's health care system would still be where it belongs, in the hands of compassionate corporations whose only interest is for the well-being of its paying customers and the profits of its shareholders.

Hillary's Fourth Lie
Of Biblical Proportions

It is easier for a camel to go through the eye
of a needle, than for a rich man to enter into
the kingdom of God

The King James Version

Mark 10

23 And Jesus looked round about, and saith unto his disciples, How hardly shall they that have riches enter into the kingdom of God!

24 And the disciples were astonished at his words. But Jesus answereth again, and saith unto them, Children, how hard is it for them that trust in riches to enter into the kingdom of God!

25 It is easier for a camel to go through the eye of a needle, than for a rich man to enter into the kingdom of God.

The New Revised Standard Version

Mark 10

23 Then Jesus looked around and said to his disciples, 'How hard it will be for those who have wealth to enter the kingdom of God!'

24And the disciples were perplexed at these words. But Jesus said to them again, 'Children, how hard it is to enter the kingdom of God!

25It is easier for a camel to go through the eye of a needle than for someone who is rich to enter the kingdom of God.'

The New Living Translation

Mark 10

23 Jesus looked around and said to his disciples, "How hard it is for the rich to enter the Kingdom of God!"

24 This amazed them. But Jesus said again, "Dear children, it is very hard to enter the Kingdom of God.

25 In fact, it is easier for a camel to go through the eye of a needle than for a rich person to enter the Kingdom of God!"

Hillary's Crooked Agenda

Hillary wants to cast doubt on my main
qualification for the highest office in the land:
I'm very rich

She wants you to believe that somehow Jesus
didn't think money was the key to salvation

Donald Trump's Truth

This is clearly a vicious attack on me personally which is, frankly very unfair. When anyone attacks me like this, I have every right to defend myself by hitting back, and hitting back hard. But first, let me give you some facts. As Christians, our faith tells us that Jesus spent his entire career as Lord and Savior working tirelessly to protect the rights of the rich, just as all Patriotic American Christians do today. And, by the way, I intend to do the same when I'm elected president with huge tax cuts for the wealthy.

Now, about Hillary: she's jealous of me because she's a loser, and I'm a winner. The only reason, and I mean the only reason she threw this crazy lie into her counterfeit Bibles was to somehow diminish the importance of my incredible success in the world of business. Sure, she's made some money over the years, not serious money like I've made, but some money. But let's face it, compared to what I've made, she's a total loser and I'm a winner – everyone knows it – I'm a winner, and I'm going to keep on winning and keep on making more money. I don't need more money; I've got plenty, but winners like me can't help it, we just keep on winning.

Let's get real: the notion that Jesus was not an ardent supporter of the rich, and in fact said that they had absolutely no shot at eternal life, is totally ridiculous.

I'm going to Heaven; I know it. Everybody knows it – everybody knows I'm going to Heaven. Look at all the work I've done and all the sacrifices I've made. I've worked hard, and built lots of buildings – very tall buildings, by the way – buildings Jesus would be very impressed with, will be very impressed with on Judgment Day.

But you know, the thing Jesus will be the most impressed with on Judgment Day is how incredibly rich I am. And there's a reason for why I'm so rich, obviously; it's because I deserve it. I'm smart – very smart – and I work hard, so hard that sometimes I'm too tired to hit back as hard as I'd like on Twitter when certain people attack me viciously – viciously and unfairly. And the press treats me unfairly as well – this we all know because the evidence is all around us every single day.

What's great about being a Christian is that I know with absolute certainty that Jesus will treat me fairly and reward my intelligence, hard work and wealth with a special place in Heaven – probably a little nicer than a lot of people get, since I've been such a big winner in this life. That's my idea of fair treatment, unlike the way the press keeps putting what I say into context to make some point or other about why I shouldn't be president – which, by the way I will be, because I deserve to be, just like I deserve to go to Heaven.

Hillary's Fifth Lie

Render unto Caesar
the things that are Caesar's

The King James Version

Mark 12

14 And when they were come, they say unto him, Master, we know that thou art true, and carest for no man: for thou regardest not the person of men, but teachest the way of God in truth: Is it lawful to give tribute to Caesar, or not?

15 Shall we give, or shall we not give? But he, knowing their hypocrisy, said unto them, Why tempt ye me? bring me a penny, that I may see [it].

16 And they brought [it]. And he saith unto them, Whose [is] this image and superscription? And they said unto him, Caesar's.

17 And Jesus answering said unto them, Render to Caesar the things that are Caesar's, and to God the things that are God's. And they marvelled at him.

The New Revised Standard Version

Mark 12

[14]And they came and said to him, 'Teacher, we know that you are sincere, and show deference to no one; for you do not regard people with partiality, but teach the way of God in accordance with truth. Is it lawful to pay taxes to the emperor, or not?

[15]Should we pay them, or should we not?' But knowing their hypocrisy, he said to them, 'Why are you putting me to the test? Bring me a denarius and let me see it.'

[16]And they brought one. Then he said to them, 'Whose head is this, and whose title?' They answered, 'The emperor's.'

[17]Jesus said to them, 'Give to the emperor the things that are the emperor's, and to God the things that are God's.' And they were utterly amazed at him.

The New Living Translation

Mark 12

¹⁴ "Teacher," they said, "we know how honest you are. You are impartial and don't play favorites. You teach the way of God truthfully. Now tell us—is it right to pay taxes to Caesar or not?

¹⁵ Should we pay them, or shouldn't we?"
  Jesus saw through their hypocrisy and said, "Why are you trying to trap me? Show me a Roman coin,* and I'll tell you."

¹⁶When they handed it to him, he asked, "Whose picture and title are stamped on it?"
  "Caesar's," they replied.

¹⁷ "Well, then," Jesus said, "give to Caesar what belongs to Caesar, and give to God what belongs to God." His reply completely amazed them.

Hillary's Crooked Agenda

What Hillary is trying to imply here is that I don't pay my fair share of taxes – which is totally ridiculous

She wants me and all other rich people to pay more taxes so her crooked government can give away quality health care and education to people who don't deserve it

Donald Trump's Truth

So here's another attack aimed directly at me. See, she wants you to believe that I don't pay my fair share of taxes – you know, rendering unto Caesar or whoever. Which is ridiculous, because I'm in the middle of an audit process now that prevents me from releasing my tax returns, but trust me, there's nothing I have ever done that isn't completely legal. I have used the law to my advantage, sure and since I'm smarter than most people, I've figured how to take full advantage of the breaks I deserve. But it's just terrible the way Hillary and her campaign staff – and let me tell you the press does this too – the way they keep hammering away at this tax return nonsense.

Now, all that hammering away hasn't done anything for them, obviously – look at my numbers in the polls. I'm so far ahead, Hillary won't ever catch up. So when their typical loser tactics didn't work, they concocted this ridiculous, totally made-up story that Jesus thought it was OK for everybody, even rich guys like me, to pay taxes to the government.

Let me break it down for you; their argument – which they falsely claim that Jesus supported – their argument is that we need taxes to support our military which, by the way is a disaster and to pay for education which in this country is also a mess, and build roads and bridges – something I could do much better than it's being done now – I build things very, very well and make a lot of money doing it, which is why I need to be president. I will build walls, roads and bridges better than anyone has ever done in the history of this country.

Hillary's crooked agenda includes devious, selfish stuff like quality health care and education for all Americans, even the ones who don't deserve it. Nobody ever asked for that. It's just her way of getting attention – and power, believe me this woman is out for power – and winning elections. I got a good education because I deserved it – I have a good brain and I was rich enough to afford it. If you want to make America great again, make sure that nobody gets anything for free. My father helped me get rich and anybody whose father doesn't do that for his loved ones doesn't really deserve a good education or quality health care, believe me they don't deserve it.

And Hillary doesn't deserve to be president. She's a loser. I'm a winner, which is why I'm so rich and I keep as much of my hard-earned money as I'm legally entitled to. It's unfair – seriously unfair – to take money from people like me who have sacrificed everything to build a very successful life – and I'm talking very, very successful – it's unfair to take the money I've earned by beating out a series of losers – one loser after another – and to take that money and throw it away in our disaster of a military is unfair, deeply unfair, I'll tell you that right now.

Hillary's Sixth Lie

Inasmuch as ye have done it unto one of the least of these my brethren, ye have done it unto me.

The King James Version

Matthew 25

[31] When the Son of man shall come in his glory, and all the holy angels with him, then shall he sit upon the throne of his glory:

[32] And before him shall be gathered all nations: and he shall separate them one from another, as a shepherd divideth [his] sheep from the goats:

[33] And he shall set the sheep on his right hand, but the goats on the left.

[34] Then shall the King say unto them on his right hand, Come, ye blessed of my Father, inherit the kingdom prepared for you from the foundation of the world:

[35] For I was an hungred, and ye gave me meat: I was thirsty, and ye gave me drink: I was a stranger, and ye took me in:

[36] Naked, and ye clothed me: I was sick, and ye visited me: I was in prison, and ye came unto me.

[37] Then shall the righteous answer him, saying, Lord, when saw we thee an hungred, and fed [thee]? or thirsty, and gave [thee] drink?

[38] When saw we thee a stranger, and took [thee] in? or naked, and clothed [thee]?

³⁹ Or when saw we thee sick, or in prison, and came unto thee?

⁴⁰ And the King shall answer and say unto them, Verily I say unto you, Inasmuch as ye have done [it] unto one of the least of these my brethren, ye have done [it] unto me.

⁴¹ Then shall he say also unto them on the left hand, Depart from me, ye cursed, into everlasting fire, prepared for the devil and his angels:

⁴² For I was an hungred, and ye gave me no meat: I was thirsty, and ye gave me no drink:

⁴³ I was a stranger, and ye took me not in: naked, and ye clothed me not: sick, and in prison, and ye visited me not.

⁴⁴ Then shall they also answer him, saying, Lord, when saw we thee an hungred, or athirst, or a stranger, or naked, or sick, or in prison, and did not minister unto thee?

⁴⁵ Then shall he answer them, saying, Verily I say unto you, Inasmuch as ye did [it] not to one of the least of these, ye did [it] not to me.

⁴⁶ And these shall go away into everlasting punishment: but the righteous into life eternal.

The New Revised Standard Version

Matthew 25

[31] 'When the Son of Man comes in his glory, and all the angels with him, then he will sit on the throne of his glory.

[32] All the nations will be gathered before him, and he will separate people one from another as a shepherd separates the sheep from the goats,

[33] and he will put the sheep at his right hand and the goats at the left.

[34] Then the king will say to those at his right hand, "Come, you that are blessed by my Father, inherit the kingdom prepared for you from the foundation of the world;

[35] for I was hungry and you gave me food, I was thirsty and you gave me something to drink, I was a stranger and you welcomed me,

[36] I was naked and you gave me clothing, I was sick and you took care of me, I was in prison and you visited me."

[37] Then the righteous will answer him, "Lord, when was it that we saw you hungry and gave you food, or thirsty and gave you something to drink?

^{38}And when was it that we saw you a stranger and welcomed you, or naked and gave you clothing?

^{39}And when was it that we saw you sick or in prison and visited you?"

^{40}And the king will answer them, "Truly I tell you, just as you did it to one of the least of these who are members of my family, you did it to me."

^{41}Then he will say to those at his left hand, "You that are accursed, depart from me into the eternal fire prepared for the devil and his angels;

^{42}for I was hungry and you gave me no food, I was thirsty and you gave me nothing to drink,

^{43}I was a stranger and you did not welcome me, naked and you did not give me clothing, sick and in prison and you did not visit me."

^{44}Then they also will answer, "Lord, when was it that we saw you hungry or thirsty or a stranger or naked or sick or in prison, and did not take care of you?"

^{45}Then he will answer them, "Truly I tell you, just as you did not do it to one of the least of these, you did not do it to me."

^{46}And these will go away into eternal punishment, but the righteous into eternal life.'

The New Living Translation

Matthew 25

[31]"But when the Son of Man comes in his glory, and all the angels with him, then he will sit upon his glorious throne.

[32] All the nations will be gathered in his presence, and he will separate the people as a shepherd separates the sheep from the goats.

[33] He will place the sheep at his right hand and the goats at his left.

[34]"Then the King will say to those on his right, 'Come, you who are blessed by my Father, inherit the Kingdom prepared for you from the creation of the world.

[35] For I was hungry, and you fed me. I was thirsty, and you gave me a drink. I was a stranger, and you invited me into your home.

[36] I was naked, and you gave me clothing. I was sick, and you cared for me. I was in prison, and you visited me.'

[37] "Then these righteous ones will reply, 'Lord, when did we ever see you hungry and feed you? Or thirsty and give you something to drink?

[38] Or a stranger and show you hospitality? Or naked and give you clothing?

[39] When did we ever see you sick or in prison and visit you?'

[40] "And the King will say, 'I tell you the truth, when you did it to one of the least of these my brothers and sisters, you were doing it to me!'

[41] "Then the King will turn to those on the left and say, 'Away with you, you cursed ones, into the eternal fire prepared for the devil and his demons.

[42] For I was hungry, and you didn't feed me. I was thirsty, and you didn't give me a drink.

[43] I was a stranger, and you didn't invite me into your home. I was naked, and you didn't give me clothing. I was sick and in prison, and you didn't visit me.'

[44] "Then they will reply, 'Lord, when did we ever see you hungry or thirsty or a stranger or naked or sick or in prison, and not help you?'

[45] "And he will answer, 'I tell you the truth, when you refused to help the least of these my brothers and sisters, you were refusing to help me.'

[46] "And they will go away into eternal punishment, but the righteous will go into eternal life."

Hillary's Crooked Agenda

Hillary wants to put you and your family in danger by inviting Muslim strangers into our country and into our homes

She's also wants to take your hard-earned money and just give it to poor people and convicted criminals

Donald Trump's Truth

This series of lies directly contradicts what I want to do for the American people. My whole purpose for running for president is to build a great big wall, which by the way I'm very good at – building tall things. Hillary doesn't have an answer for that except to tell that lie that I can't do it, which of course I can, and that the Mexicans won't ever pay for it, which of course they will. Believe me, I can force them to pay for that wall.

So since she has no real answer to my plan to build this wall that, trust me, will be visible from space, she throws in this ridiculous passage in language that's supposed to sound somehow Biblical, to make her gullible fans believe that Jesus wanted us to welcome strangers, which is totally ridiculous. Think about it. America is a Christian nation and if Jesus wanted us to let immigrants in, we would have been doing it for the past 200 years, which we obviously haven't.

But here's the real kicker on this thing. See, not only does she make up this story about Jesus liking immigrants, but in the same little story, tells us that he likes criminals, too – did you see that thing about visiting convicts in prison? That's a clear – and I mean very clear endorsement of the Mexican criminal element that has been flooding over our southern borders since Barack Obama took office.

The really clever – crooked but clever, and I admire cleverness, believe me, I know cleverness when I see it – the really clever thing Hillary does here is to take two of my most important plans and tries to make them both un-Christian with the same made-up, ridiculous nonsense that Jesus was supposed to have said – which of course we know he didn't – about welcoming strangers. Let me ask you, besides Mexicans, who else would you consider strangers? Muslims, of course, and we know that Muslims hate America and want to destroy us.

Now ask yourself, why would both Barack Obama and Hillary Clinton want to let a bunch of terrorists into our country? Something is going on here, folks, and we all know what that is – I don't need to say it out loud; we all know what's going on here. And what better way to help their terrorist friends get into America and kill us all than to stick some outrageous lie into our Bible – the actual Holy Bible, it's really unbelievable – about welcoming strangers into our home: the United States of America.

The icing on the cake – and of course she would do this – is falsely quoting Jesus as saying that the people who let Muslim terrorists and Mexican rapists into our beautiful country will go to Heaven and that people like me who want to keep them out will burn in hell, which is totally ridiculous to think a good Christian like myself would not get into Heaven.

Hillary's Seventh Lie

Sell that thou hast and give to the poor

The King James Version

Matthew 19

16 And, behold, one came and said unto him, Good Master, what good thing shall I do, that I may have eternal life?

17 And he said unto him, Why callest thou me good? [there is] none good but one, [that is], God: but if thou wilt enter into life, keep the commandments.

18 He saith unto him, Which? Jesus said, Thou shalt do no murder, Thou shalt not commit adultery, Thou shalt not steal, Thou shalt not bear false witness,

19 Honour thy father and [thy] mother: and, Thou shalt love thy neighbour as thyself.

20 The young man saith unto him, All these things have I kept from my youth up: what lack I yet?

21 Jesus said unto him, If thou wilt be perfect, go [and] sell that thou hast, and give to the poor, and thou shalt have treasure in heaven: and come [and] follow me.

22 But when the young man heard that saying, he went away sorrowful: for he had great possessions.

The New Revised Standard Version

Matthew 19

16 Then someone came to him and said, 'Teacher, what good deed must I do to have eternal life?'

17And he said to him, 'Why do you ask me about what is good? There is only one who is good. If you wish to enter into life, keep the commandments.'

18He said to him, 'Which ones?' And Jesus said, 'You shall not murder; You shall not commit adultery; You shall not steal; You shall not bear false witness;

19Honour your father and mother; also, You shall love your neighbour as yourself.'

20The young man said to him, 'I have kept all these;* what do I still lack?'

21Jesus said to him, 'If you wish to be perfect, go, sell your possessions, and give the money* to the poor, and you will have treasure in heaven; then come, follow me.'

22When the young man heard this word, he went away grieving, for he had many possessions.

The New Living Translation

Matthew 19

[16] Someone came to Jesus with this question: "Teacher, what good deed must I do to have eternal life?"

[17] "Why ask me about what is good?" Jesus replied. "There is only One who is good. But to answer your question—if you want to receive eternal life, keep the commandments."

[18] "Which ones?" the man asked.
And Jesus replied: "'You must not murder. You must not commit adultery. You must not steal. You must not testify falsely.

[19] Honor your father and mother. Love your neighbor as yourself.'"

[20]"I've obeyed all these commandments," the young man replied. "What else must I do?"

[21] Jesus told him, "If you want to be perfect, go and sell all your possessions and give the money to the poor, and you will have treasure in heaven. Then come, follow me."

[22]But when the young man heard this, he went away sad, for he had many possessions.

Hillary's Crooked Agenda

Here she goes attacking me for the thing that I
do best – making money

The hidden agenda – and there is always a
hidden agenda with this one – is to get me and
my fellow winners to give our money to lazy,
stupid losers

Donald Trump's Truth

Hillary and her campaign staff actually want us to believe Jesus – that's Jesus Christ – said that in order to get into Heaven, we're supposed to give up all we've worked so hard for and give it to some deadbeat welfare mother. Now clearly, clearly there's something really wrong with that. I mean, first of all Jesus obviously never said anything remotely like that. Secondly: there's a reason they're the poor Actually there are two reasons:

1. They're a bunch of losers
2. If God had wanted them to be rich, they'd already be rich

It's so obvious: God wants the rich to be rich, or they wouldn't be rich – or in my case very, very rich. Since we know that, why would anyone believe that His son would go around telling the very people he has blessed with wealth – in my case enormous wealth – to give the fruits of their labor to the undeserving poor?

You see where I'm going with this, right? Planting the notion that Jesus would want rich people to give their money to the poor is just a transparent strategy from the Clinton campaign to raise taxes on the winners, like me, and give our money to stupid losers who wouldn't know what to do with money even if they had it. Believe me they wouldn't have a clue what to do with my money.

So don't be naïve, folks. Jesus Christ never told anybody to give away their money. And the only reason Hillary is preaching this ridiculous nonsense is that it gets her votes. See, there are a lot more poor people than there are rich people – winners like me are very few compared to the huge numbers of losers out there in America.

So for Hillary to get elected, she needs to pander – I mean shamelessly suck up to the losers who didn't bother to get rich like I did. Believe me, I've made some huge sacrifices to get as rich as I am. You wouldn't believe the sacrifices I've made to get as rich and powerful, tremendously powerful as I am now. Meanwhile all Hillary needs to do is get all those losers all riled up about this so-called income inequality so she can stay employed by a government that's so screwed up – and believe me it's totally screwed up – great leaders like Vladimir Putin and would never tolerate how screwed up America is.

Like every patriotic American, I keep every bit of my money for myself. That's what America is all about, right? America is about the freedom to win big deals and rub the losers' noses in it when it's all over. Jesus would be doing the same thing if he was alive today, believe me.

Hillary's Eighth Lie

Love thy neighbor as thyself

The King James Version

Luke 10

[25] And, behold, a certain lawyer stood up, and tempted him, saying, Master, what shall I do to inherit eternal life?

[26] He said unto him, What is written in the law? how readest thou?

[27] And he answering said, Thou shalt love the Lord thy God with all thy heart, and with all thy soul, and with all thy strength, and with all thy mind; and thy neighbour as thyself.

[28] And he said unto him, Thou hast answered right: this do, and thou shalt live.

The New Revised Standard Version

Luke 10

25 Just then a lawyer stood up to test Jesus. 'Teacher,' he said, 'what must I do to inherit eternal life?'

26He said to him, 'What is written in the law? What do you read there?'

27He answered, 'You shall love the Lord your God with all your heart, and with all your soul, and with all your strength, and with all your mind; and your neighbour as yourself.'

28And he said to him, 'You have given the right answer; do this, and you will live.'

The New Living Translation

Luke 10

25 One day an expert in religious law stood up to test Jesus by asking him this question: "Teacher, what should I do to inherit eternal life?"

26 Jesus replied, "What does the law of Moses say? How do you read it?"

27 The man answered, "'You must love the Lord your God with all your heart, all your soul, all your strength, and all your mind.' And, 'Love your neighbor as yourself.'"

28 "Right!" Jesus told him. "Do this and you will live!"

Hillary's Crooked Agenda

She clearly wants you to interpret the word
"neighbor" to mean Mexican rapist

Once she opens the borders to every criminal
the Mexican government wants to send us,
she thinks they'll vote for her and keep her in
that cushy government job she likes so much

Then she will destroy America's slave-wage
job market by giving dead-end jobs to these
murderers so they can carry on their killing
spree in comfort and security

Donald Trump's Truth

Here's another attempt to undermine the most important mission of my campaign – building a great wall to keep the Mexican government from sending the dregs – and I mean the lowest of the low – the Mexican government has been systematically sending worst criminals they have across our southern border and I alone can stop them. See, I build things, very big, very impressive things like casinos and skyscrapers and so I know how to build things, believe me, and I know how to build a wall. And by the way I'm the only one who could get the Mexican government to pay for this very impressive wall.

So along comes the Hillary Clinton campaign issuing these counterfeit Bibles with ridiculous, total nonsense that's supposed to be the words of our Lord and Savior. But it's easy, so easy to see right through this lie: love your "neighbor" as yourself, as if you can't tell from her anti-American agenda that by "neighbor" she means "Mexican rapist".

If we were to actually love these foreigners as ourselves, we'd be giving them opportunities that God clearly doesn't want them to have. He, God, obviously doesn't want Mexicans to have the same opportunities as Americans because they were born in Mexico, and God's in charge of who gets born where.

Hillary's Ninth Lie

The Story of the Good Samaritan

The King James Version - Luke 10

29 But he, willing to justify himself, said unto Jesus, And who is my neighbour?

30 And Jesus answering said, A certain [man] went down from Jerusalem to Jericho, and fell among thieves, which stripped him of his raiment, and wounded [him], and departed, leaving [him] half dead.

31 And by chance there came down a certain priest that way: and when he saw him, he passed by on the other side.

32 And likewise a Levite, when he was at the place, came and looked [on him], and passed by on the other side.

33 But a certain Samaritan, as he journeyed, came where he was: and when he saw him, he had compassion [on him],

34 And went to [him], and bound up his wounds, pouring in oil and wine, and set him on his own beast, and brought him to an inn, and took care of him.

35 And on the morrow when he departed, he took out two pence, and gave [them] to the host, and said unto him, Take care of him; and whatsoever thou spendest more, when I come again, I will repay thee.

36 Which now of these three, thinkest thou, was neighbour unto him that fell among the thieves?

37 And he said, He that shewed mercy on him. Then said Jesus unto him, Go, and do thou likewise.

The New Revised Standard Version - Luke 10

[29]But wanting to justify himself, he asked Jesus, 'And who is my neighbour?'

[30]Jesus replied, 'A man was going down from Jerusalem to Jericho, and fell into the hands of robbers, who stripped him, beat him, and went away, leaving him half dead.

[31]Now by chance a priest was going down that road; and when he saw him, he passed by on the other side.

[32]So likewise a Levite, when he came to the place and saw him, passed by on the other side.

[33]But a Samaritan while travelling came near him; and when he saw him, he was moved with pity.

[34]He went to him and bandaged his wounds, having poured oil and wine on them. Then he put him on his own animal, brought him to an inn, and took care of him.

[35]The next day he took out two denarii, gave them to the innkeeper, and said, "Take care of him; and when I come back, I will repay you whatever more you spend."

[36]Which of these three, do you think, was a neighbour to the man who fell into the hands of the robbers?'

[37]He said, 'The one who showed him mercy.' Jesus said to him, 'Go and do likewise.'

The New Living Translation - Luke 10

29 The man wanted to justify his actions, so he asked Jesus, "And who is my neighbor?"

30 Jesus replied with a story: "A Jewish man was traveling from Jerusalem down to Jericho, and he was attacked by bandits. They stripped him of his clothes, beat him up, and left him half dead beside the road.

31 "By chance a priest came along. But when he saw the man lying there, he crossed to the other side of the road and passed him by.

32 A Temple assistant walked over and looked at him lying there, but he also passed by on the other side.

33 "Then a despised Samaritan came along, and when he saw the man, he felt compassion for him

34 Going over to him, the Samaritan soothed his wounds with olive oil and wine and bandaged them. Then he put the man on his own donkey and took him to an inn, where he took care of him.

35 The next day he handed the innkeeper two silver coins, telling him, 'Take care of this man. If his bill runs higher than this, I'll pay you the next time I'm here.'

36 "Now which of these three would you say was a neighbor to the man who was attacked by bandits?" Jesus asked.

37 The man replied, "The one who showed him mercy."

Then Jesus said, "Yes, now go and do the same."

Hillary's Crooked Agenda

Treat Muslims and Mexicans as if they might actually be good people capable of making positive contributions to America

It's all for the votes, people, it's all for the votes

Donald Trump's Truth

So now the Clinton campaign is trying to support their ridiculous claim – and it is totally ridiculous, as any Bible scholar can tell you – the ridiculous claim that Jesus said loving our "neighbors" is the key to eternal life. So they come up with this "parable" that supposedly tells us that foreigners, like Muslims and Mexicans can actually do something good – actual good for natural-born citizens. As if any Muslim has ever done anything good for Americans. You tell me – has any Muslim ever done anything good for you? I don't know, maybe, but I've never seen this happen.

Sure, a Muslim soldier died in Iraq – but let me tell you, a guy who dies is not my idea of a war hero. Guys who die and guys who get taken prisoner are not heroes, they're losers. The real heroes are the ones – and I'm very serious here – the real heroes are the ones who win battles, who win medals and who live to fight another day. And the real heroes are not the guys whose parents viciously attack a man – and yes, I was viciously attacked and have every right to defend myself – heroes are not the guys whose parents viciously attack a man who is trying to make America great again.

People, don't believe for a minute that Jesus actually believed that Muslims and Mexicans – and this passage uses Samaritans as proxies for Muslims and Mexicans, which is very clever, but totally transparent and totally ridiculous – that Muslims and Mexicans are capable of acts of kindness toward natural-born citizens. You know it, I know it, these people are up to no good and we need to close our borders and send these criminals back where they came from. You know this, I know this, Jesus would have done the same, but Hillary and her crooked staff have actually stooped to creating these crazy counterfeit stories to try and get the Christian vote.

I have people who looked into these counterfeit Bibles – really great people with credentials you wouldn't believe – and these people assure me that the ridiculous stuff the Clinton people stuck into these Bibles is clearly targeted at me, personally. And this "Good Samaritan" article is a perfect example of how devious these people are.

It's pretty easy to see, though, when you're as good at understanding conspiracy as I am – and I'm very, very good at recognizing a conspiracy when I see it – it's pretty easy to see what they're doing here. They're trying to say that I'm like all the people who didn't help that loser who was lying on the side of the road, and that some Muslim fanatic would actually stop and help this guy – who by the way shouldn't have gotten his butt kicked in the first place.

See, America is about winners, not losers. It's about real heroes, not victims and prisoners. If I interrupted my day every time some loser got his butt kicked – and believe me, losers get their butts kicked all day long – I wouldn't have any time, any time at all to accomplish all the truly great things I've achieved in my life.

Hillary's Tenth Lie

Neither hath this man sinned, nor his parents

The King James Version

John 9

1 And as [Jesus] passed by, he saw a man which was blind from [his] birth.

2 And his disciples asked him, saying, Master, who did sin, this man, or his parents, that he was born blind?

3 Jesus answered, Neither hath this man sinned, nor his parents: but that the works of God should be made manifest in him.

4 I must work the works of him that sent me, while it is day: the night cometh, when no man can work.

5 As long as I am in the world, I am the light of the world.

6 When he had thus spoken, he spat on the ground, and made clay of the spittle, and he anointed the eyes of the blind man with the clay,

7 And said unto him, Go, wash in the pool of Siloam, (which is by interpretation, Sent.) He went his way therefore, and washed, and came seeing.

The New Revised Standard Version

John 9

[1]As he walked along, he saw a man blind from birth.

[2]His disciples asked him, 'Rabbi, who sinned, this man or his parents, that he was born blind?'

[3]Jesus answered, 'Neither this man nor his parents sinned; he was born blind so that God's works might be revealed in him.

[4]We must work the works of him who sent me while it is day; night is coming when no one can work.

[5]As long as I am in the world, I am the light of the world.'

[6]When he had said this, he spat on the ground and made mud with the saliva and spread the mud on the man's eyes,

[7]saying to him, 'Go, wash in the pool of Siloam' (which means Sent). Then he went and washed and came back able to see.

The New Living Translation

John 9

¹ As Jesus was walking along, he saw a man who had been blind from birth.

² "Rabbi," his disciples asked him, "why was this man born blind? Was it because of his own sins or his parents' sins?"

³"It was not because of his sins or his parents' sins," Jesus answered. "This happened so the power of God could be seen in him.

⁴ We must quickly carry out the tasks assigned us by the one who sent us. The night is coming, and then no one can work.

⁵ But while I am here in the world, I am the light of the world."

⁶ Then he spit on the ground, made mud with the saliva, and spread the mud over the blind man's eyes.

⁷ He told him, "Go wash yourself in the pool of Siloam" (Siloam means "sent"). So the man went and washed and came back seeing!

Hillary's Crooked Agenda

She wants to justify Obamacare which
provides health care coverage to the
undeserving poor, Muslims and Mexicans
even when they have pre-existing conditions

Donald Trump's Truth

OK, let's get real here. First of all, this little story – which by the way is totally false, totally fabricated – is a shameless endorsement of Obamacare. You'll notice, first of all that Jesus doesn't ask to get paid for curing this guy – which by the way is what our supposed allies in NATO are doing to us – getting us to fix their problems without paying for it. But Jesus not getting paid for curing this loser is just what we're doing with this ridiculous Obamacare.

Hillary wants to continue that disaster of a health care bill that was started by that disaster of a president – who as we all know isn't even a citizen and is definitely not a Christian – she wants to keep that train-wreck of a system in place for another 4 years. She wants to provide health care for people who don't deserve it, didn't earn it and come into the system with pre-existing conditions, like this blind loser Jesus is supposed to have cured for free.

Now let me tell you something; let me tell you something: Jesus did NOT work for free, he did not work for free. I have people, very good people, the best people, who know everything, everything there is to know about the real Bible and they have assured me that Jesus NEVER worked for free. He was, my people have told me – and this is something Hillary's people don't want you to know – they have told me that our Lord and Savior was actually a very, very successful entrepreneur, much like myself. He built a spiritual healing empire across Palestine and Judea the likes of which nobody had ever seen – very, very successful guy, this Jesus of Nazareth.

Based on these facts, it's insane to think that Jesus would have healed this guy for nothing in return. But what makes me so mad is that part about this loser not being a sinner and – get this – his parents weren't sinners either. In other words – and this is the personal attack that gets me so, you know, I just want to hit back so hard – in other words instead of deporting the children of Mexican rapists like I said we should, she's saying that we should give them free health care, like her fictional version of Jesus did.

And now here's the icing on the cake. The blind guy was born blind; talk about your pre-existing conditions! No self-respecting businessman – and Jesus Christ was a very successful businessman believe me – no business person in his right mind would take on a client who was already in trouble. I know this and have applied it to my own life on many, many occasions. See nobody would lend me money if they believed I was in trouble, so I was never, never stupid enough to let the lenders see that I had a problem paying back loans – never. If the blind guy wasn't such a loser, he would have pretended to be able to see. But this is a made-up story in a phony version of our Holy Scripture, so all bets are off. Since this fictional Jesus didn't ask for money anyway – which we all know he did; Jesus didn't work for free – since this fake Jesus wasn't going to ask the blind guy for money anyway, there wasn't any reason for him to be smart enough to lie about his condition. The whole thing is totally ridiculous.

So with the "neither has this man sinned" nonsense they covered giving health care away for free, and they covered pre-existing conditions, but they had to create another total fabrication – like all of these fake Bible verses – they made up one more story to cover the bums. Check out this one about how Christ heals a blind bum he finds on the street:

King James Version - Luke 18

35 And it came to pass, that as he was come nigh unto Jericho, a certain blind man sat by the way side begging:

36 And hearing the multitude pass by, he asked what it meant.

37 And they told him, that Jesus of Nazareth passeth by.

38 And he cried, saying, Jesus, Son of David, have mercy on me.

39 And they which went before rebuked him, that he should hold his peace: but he cried so much the more, Son of David, have mercy on me.

40 And Jesus stood, and commanded him to be brought unto him: and when he was come near, he asked him,

⁴¹ Saying, What wilt thou that I shall do unto thee? And he said, Lord, that I may receive my sight.

⁴² And Jesus said unto him, Receive thy sight: thy faith hath saved thee.

⁴³ And immediately he received his sight, and followed him, glorifying God: and all the people, when they saw [it], gave praise unto God.

This is no way to run a country – we can't give free health care to bums and expect to prosper as a nation.

Hillary's Eleventh Lie

Do unto others
as you would have others do unto you

The King James Version

Matthew 7

[9] Or what man is there of you, whom if his son ask bread, will he give him a stone?

[10] Or if he ask a fish, will he give him a serpent?

[11] If ye then, being evil, know how to give good gifts unto your children, how much more shall your Father which is in heaven give good things to them that ask him?

[12] Therefore all things whatsoever ye would that men should do to you, do ye even so to them: for this is the law and the prophets.

The New Revised Standard Version

Matthew 7

[9]Is there anyone among you who, if your child asks for bread, will give a stone?

[10]Or if the child asks for a fish, will give a snake?

[11]If you then, who are evil, know how to give good gifts to your children, how much more will your Father in heaven give good things to those who ask him!

[12] 'In everything do to others as you would have them do to you; for this is the law and the prophets.

The New Living Translation

Matthew 7

[9] "You parents—if your children ask for a loaf of bread, do you give them a stone instead?

[10] Or if they ask for a fish, do you give them a snake? Of course not!

[11] So if you sinful people know how to give good gifts to your children, how much more will your heavenly Father give good gifts to those who ask him.

[12] "Do to others whatever you would like them to do to you. This is the essence of all that is taught in the law and the prophets.

Hillary's Crooked Agenda

She wants to cast me as some kind of mean, nasty person instead of the truly remarkable winner that I really am

Donald Trump's Truth

This one crosses the line from the ridiculous to the totally absurd. Winners don't talk like this, and believe me Jesus was a winner – I mean, we're still talking about him 2,000 years later, just like people will be talking about me 2,000 years from now. See, winners do unto others BEFORE others do unto them. They do it unto them harder, faster and smarter, because the world is full of winners and losers, and believe me if others did unto me like I do unto them, I'd hit back so hard it would make their heads spin, trust me, their heads would spin.

Hillary wants me to treat the losers the way they treat me, which is totally absurd, because that would make them winners and make me a loser. She wants me to be a loser, so her crooked campaign staff created this outrageous lie about Jesus treating losers like winners and that's just nuts. A winner like our Lord and Savior – and he was a major winner, believe me – Jesus would never be stupid enough to treat losers like winners. He was a smart guy, very smart guy and he knew as well as I do that when you treat losers like winners, only the winners lose. I don't treat losers like winners, and I never, never lose – believe me, I never lose. And if I do, I'll sue the loser who beats me so fast that he's the loser anyway – I don't lose.

Now let me give you some examples that demonstrate exactly how totally absurd this do unto others thing is – and it really is totally absurd. If we actually did unto others what we want them to do unto us:

We would create economic conditions favorable to the poor, to artists, and to public sector employees like school teachers and police officers, *just because* we want conditions favorable to *our* economic interests.

We would stop using enhanced interrogation techniques *just because* we wouldn't want waterboarding done unto us.

We would improve the quality of education for children in poor urban communities and rural America, for the children of immigrants and single working mothers with two full-time jobs, *just because* we want a quality education for our own children.

We would respect the religious beliefs of Godless Muslims *just because* we want our own religious beliefs to be respected.

We would support quality health care for the undeserving poor, the retired and the self-employed *just because* we want that very thing for ourselves and our families.

This would obviously be a ridiculous way to live.

Hillary's Twelfth Lie

Let he who is without sin cast the first stone

The King James Version - John 8

1 Jesus went unto the mount of Olives.

2 And early in the morning he came again into the temple, and all the people came unto him; and he sat down, and taught them.

3 And the scribes and Pharisees brought unto him a woman taken in adultery; and when they had set her in the midst,

4 They say unto him, Master, this woman was taken in adultery, in the very act.

5 Now Moses in the law commanded us, that such should be stoned: but what sayest thou?

6 This they said, tempting him, that they might have to accuse him. But Jesus stooped down, and with [his] finger wrote on the ground, [as though he heard them not].

7 So when they continued asking him, he lifted up himself, and said unto them, He that is without sin among you, let him first cast a stone at her.

8 And again he stooped down, and wrote on the ground.

9 And they which heard [it], being convicted by [their own] conscience, went out one by one, beginning at the eldest, [even] unto the last: and Jesus was left alone, and the woman standing in the midst.

10 When Jesus had lifted up himself, and saw none but the woman, he said unto her, Woman, where are those thine accusers? hath no man condemned thee?

11 She said, No man, Lord. And Jesus said unto her, Neither do I condemn thee: go, and sin no more.

The New Revised Standard Version
John 8

[1]Jesus went to the Mount of Olives.

[2]Early in the morning he came again to the temple. All the people came to him and he sat down and began to teach them.

[3]The scribes and the Pharisees brought a woman who had been caught in adultery; and making her stand before all of them,

[4]they said to him, 'Teacher, this woman was caught in the very act of committing adultery.

[5]Now in the law Moses commanded us to stone such women. Now what do you say?'

[6]They said this to test him, so that they might have some charge to bring against him. Jesus bent down and wrote with his finger on the ground.

[7]When they kept on questioning him, he straightened up and said to them, 'Let anyone among you who is without sin be the first to throw a stone at her.'

[8]And once again he bent down and wrote on the ground.[*]

[9]When they heard it, they went away, one by one, beginning with the elders; and Jesus was left alone with the woman standing before him.

[10]Jesus straightened up and said to her, 'Woman, where are they? Has no one condemned you?'

[11]She said, 'No one, sir.'[*] And Jesus said, 'Neither do I condemn you. Go your way, and from now on do not sin again.'

The New Living Translation
John 8

[1] Jesus returned to the Mount of Olives,

[2] but early the next morning he was back again at the Temple. A crowd soon gathered, and he sat down and taught them.

[3] As he was speaking, the teachers of religious law and the Pharisees brought a woman who had been caught in the act of adultery. They put her in front of the crowd.

[4] "Teacher," they said to Jesus, "this woman was caught in the act of adultery.

[5] The law of Moses says to stone her. What do you say?"

[6] They were trying to trap him into saying something they could use against him, but Jesus stooped down and wrote in the dust with his finger.

[7] They kept demanding an answer, so he stood up again and said, "All right, but let the one who has never sinned throw the first stone!"

[8] Then he stooped down again and wrote in the dust.

[9] When the accusers heard this, they slipped away one by one, beginning with the oldest, until only Jesus was left in the middle of the crowd with the woman.

[10] Then Jesus stood up again and said to the woman, "Where are your accusers? Didn't even one of them condemn you?"

[11] "No, Lord," she said And Jesus said, "Neither do I. Go and sin no more."

Hillary's Crooked Agenda

She wants to reward criminals, especially Mexican criminals and create a lawless, violent society by eliminating the death penalty

Donald Trump's Truth

This is the Clinton Campaign's full-on attack against my strong, aggressive, totally American stance on law-and order. See, this woman had it coming. She had committed a crime – and adultery is a terrible crime for a woman to commit; it's different for a man, of course. If I had an affair while I was a married man, that's my business and mine alone – end of story.

Anyway, crime needs to be punished, and when you look at this ridiculous, totally fabricated story that is supposedly in the Bible, it's about abolishing punishment and it's about abolishing the death penalty. Now it should be obvious that this passage was not part of the original Bible, because when you look at all the other things Jesus said about the importance of vengeance, and punishment – when you look at the number of times he told his followers to hit back hard, it's so clear that this story about forgiving this criminal is just another of Hillary's made-up verses to justify her soft-on-crime attitude. Hillary wants to make sure that Mexican criminals continue to roam free – and they're roaming free now, believe me – they want these criminals to roam free so they can continue murdering, raping and terrorizing you and your loved ones.

Believe me, the death penalty is a good thing – a very, very good thing – and it should be brought back and brought back strong. It should be the foundation of law and order in our country as a reminder to criminals that harsh, Christian punishment will be the price for coming across the border and committing crime in America.

ABOUT THE AUTHOR

Donald Trump is a true American Christian, according to public statements he has made. This book, which he didn't write a single word of, is a sincere exploration of his religious values in the context of his candidacy for the presidency of the United States as imagined by a writer who has never actually met or spoken with him. The author has actually read some of the Bible and has been an admirer of Jesus since early childhood. He sincerely hopes that this volume sheds some light on Trump's claim that he is a Christian.